Read & Respond

FOR KS2

SECTION 1

The Butterfly Lion
Teachers' notes 3

SECTION 2

Guided reading
Teachers' notes 4

SECTION 3

Shared reading
Shared reading.. 7
Photocopiable extracts........................... 8

SECTION 4

Plot, character and setting
Activity notes 11
Photocopiable sheets 15

SECTION 5

Talk about it
Activity notes 19
Photocopiable activities........................ 22

SECTION 6

Get writing
Activity notes 25
Photocopiable activities........................ 28

SECTION 7

Assessment
Teachers' notes and activity 31
Photocopiable activity 32

Read & Respond

FOR KS2

Author: Chris Lutrario

Development Editor: Simret Brar

Editor: Roanne Charles

Assistant Editor: Jo Kemp

Series Designer: Anna Oliwa

Designer: Q2A Media

Illustrations: Christian Birmingham

Text © 2008 Chris Lutrario © 2008 Scholastic Ltd

Designed using Adobe InDesign
Published by Scholastic Ltd, Villiers House,
Clarendon Avenue, Leamington Spa,
Warwickshire CV32 5PR
www.scholastic.co.uk

Printed by Bell & Bain
2 3 4 5 6 7 8 9   8 9 0 1 2 3 4 5 6 7
British Library Cataloguing-in-Publication Data
A catalogue record for this book is available from the British
Library.
ISBN 978-0439-94582-0

Acknowledgements

The publishers gratefully acknowledge permission to reproduce the following copyright material: **Christian Birmingham** for the re-use of illustrations from *The Butterfly Lion* by Michael Morpurgo Illustrations © 1996, Christian Birmingham (1996, HarperCollins Children's Books). **HarperCollins Publishers Ltd** for the use of extracts and the front cover of *The Butterfly Lion* by Michael Morpurgo. Text © 1996, Michael Morpurgo. Cover © 2007, HarperCollins Publishers. Cover photographs lion cub © Martin Harvey, Gallo Images/CORBIS, Savanna Royalty free CORBIS (Cover 2007, HarperCollins Children's books) (Text, 1996, HarperCollins Children's Books). Every effort has been made to trace copyright holders for the works reproduced in this book, and the publishers apologise for any inadvertent omissions.

About the book

The book consists of a series of closely interwoven stories that cover a wide span of historical periods and geographical locations. The stories are told in the first person by two narrators. The first of these narrators, looking back at his boyhood, describes how he ran away from boarding school and met Millie, an old lady living on her own in a big dilapidated house. In the long central part of the book she becomes narrator, telling her visitor about 'her Bertie': about his childhood on a farm in Africa; how he brings an orphaned white lion cub to live with the family; how he is sent to England and, like the first narrator, runs away from school; his bravery on the battlefields of France during the First World War; how he is reunited with the white lion and returns with it to England. In the last two chapters, the first narrator resumes the story, recounting how Millie persuaded him to return to school, where he learns more about Bertie and about Millie herself.

Throughout, much is left for the reader to puzzle out, in particular the relationship between Bertie and Millie (they were husband and wife), the identity of the boy/narrator (he is named late on as 'Morpurgo'), and the nature of the 'butterfly lion' (the figure of a lion carved by Bertie and Millie on a chalk hillside and sometimes covered with a cloud of blue butterflies). At the end of the story, the boy learns that the old lady has been dead for some time – a discovery that throws into question the reality of his meeting with her. What remains clear is that her story has a special power for him and changes his life.

The novel combines elements of adventure and mystery in thought-provoking and engaging ways. At its centre are themes of loneliness, freedom and commitment. It offers ideal material for use in the Year 3 unit on adventure and mystery and Year 4 units focused on stories with historical settings and stories that raise issues or dilemmas.

About the author

Michael Morpurgo was born in St Albans in 1943. He attended schools in London, Sussex and Kent and studied English and French at London University. Before taking up a career as a writer, he taught in a primary school. He was awarded the MBE in 1999 and the OBE in 2006, and served as Children's Laureate from 2003 to 2005.

He is the author of over a hundred books for children. Among the most well-known and well-loved are *The Wreck of the Zanzibar, Out of the Ashes, Kensuke's Kingdom* and *Private Peaceful*. In 1976, Michael and his wife Clare set up Farms for City Children, a charity that aims to provide children from inner-city areas with an experience of the countryside and rural life.

Michael Morpurgo is a high-profile and active figure in the world of children's literature and in children's lives and education more generally.

> **Facts and figures**
> *The Butterfly Lion:*
> First published: 1996
> Available as an audio book read by the author and Virgina Mckenna, whose work was an inspiration for the book.
> Winner the Smarties Prize and the Writer's Guild Award for children's fiction.

Guided reading

Chilblains and Semolina Pudding and Strange Meeting

These first two chapters recount how the boy narrator (later to be identified as 'Morpurgo') runs away from the boarding school where he is so miserable and comes to meet an old lady (later to be identified as Millie).

Focusing on the first page, ask the children about the many questions it raises for the reader: *What is the butterfly lion? Who is telling the story? Why mustn't he forget? Who is 'them' referred to in the last line?* Discuss why the author holds back this information; how it arouses the reader's curiosity and encourages reading on, and prompts active involvement.

Check that the children understand the less-familiar words used in describing the boarding school (on page 8) and talk about the way that they provide clues that the action here takes place in the past.

Identify and talk about the difficult decisions that the boy makes (to run away, to change his plan, to go with the old lady).

Review further questions that these chapters raise: *Who is Bertie? Who is the old lady? Why is there a lion shape on the hillside? Why/how does it change colour? What does it have to do with Bertie and the old lady?*

Timbavati (to the end of page 26)

The first seven pages of this chapter (up to 'One evening…' on page 26) provide a general description of the life of Bertie and his parents on a farm in Africa.

It would be helpful here to provide some background information about Britain's colonial past and to check that the children understand the subject-specific vocabulary, such as 'compound', 'veld', 'impala', 'malaria' and 'kopje'.

Identify the problems that the family faces and the impact these have on Bertie.

Prompt the children to begin to build up a picture of Bertie. *What can we tell so far about what kind of child he is?* Note in particular his loneliness, determination and longing for freedom.

Examine the structure of the story and ask: *Who is telling the story now?* (No longer the boy of the first two chapters, but the old lady.)

Remainder of Timbavati to the end of Bertie and the Lion

In this section, the old lady describes Bertie's encounter with the white lion.

Look at the phrase 'One evening' and draw out the idea that this marks the end of the scene-setting description and begins the recounting of the specific action or event.

Ask the children to identify the main incidents in order, and to relate them to Bertie's feelings and reactions. Help the children with ideas by asking: *When is he excited? Miserable? Brave? Surprised? Happy?*

Now bring these thoughts together by asking: *What more do we know about Bertie now we have heard about this event?*

Prompt the children to consider also the personalities of his father and mother and Bertie's relationships with them. *Why do you think his mother says about the lion cub, "He needs us, and maybe we need him"? How does the lion change their lives?*

Running Free

Pause in the reading of this chapter to encourage children to speculate about what might happen next and to focus on how the story is being told.

After the first paragraph, ask: *Why do you think the author tells us that the year ends 'painfully'? What effect does this have on the way we read on?* On page 47, pause after 'stepped out into the night' and ask: *What do you think Bertie is going to do? Why has he taken the gun with him?*

Guided reading

At the end of the chapter, review the decisions made by Bertie and by his father, and how the situation has changed for the family. Note the title of the chapter, and ask: *Who is running free now?* (The lion.) *Who is not?* (Bertie is trapped in various ways.)

The Frenchman

This chapter continues the story of Bertie and the lion. See if the children remember who is telling this story and to whom.

Explore the way the author presents Bertie's father and the Frenchman: are they villains, 'baddies'? Elicit that they are not presented as all bad and challenge the children to find evidence of their good points. For example, Bertie's father does not actually 'strap' him, and has previously relented about keeping the lion; the circus owner is 'earnest and trustworthy' and promises to treat the lion well. *Why does this 'not make Bertie feel any better'?* (He wants the lion to be free.)

Strawbridge and And All's Well

Read the first paragraph of 'Strawbridge' and ask the children who is telling the story now. (Not the old lady, but the boy again.) *Where are we now?* (No longer in Africa, but back in the old lady's kitchen and in the present.)

Move on to the point at which the old lady resumes her story, and ask: *Who is 'I'?* (The old lady.) *Why does she use 'I' now?* (She is directly involved in the story.)

She goes on, in the rest of this chapter and the next, to describe her childhood, her meeting with Bertie and their friendship, up to his departure to fight in the First World War. Explore this episode with the children by asking: *What do Bertie and young Millie have in common?* (Both are lonely only children living confined lives.) *What do Bertie and the boy have in common?* (They went to the same school and met Millie as they were

running away from it.) *What do we learn about Bertie and Millie?*

Note in particular the growing friendship between them, the impact of Bertie's stories about Africa on Millie, his continued desire for freedom – he feels trapped inside the walls of the college and joins up as a way of escape. *How much time passes?* (About six years: the characters are ten at the start of this episode and at the end Bertie is old enough to join up.)

A Lot of Old Codswallop

Note another brief interlude before the old lady continues her story by recounting her and Bertie's wartime experiences. Focusing on the first paragraph of this, ask the children what they learn about Bertie and Millie. (Bertie survived the war and they continued a relationship.) Note that the author holds back details about the nature of this relationship. Examine how the carefully phased presentation of information keeps the reader involved and curious.

Focus on the passage on pages 83–6 that describes how Bertie rescues two wounded comrades. Let the children identify powerful, expressive verbs that the author uses to make this vivid and exciting.

Ask the children to identify what Millie says to Bertie when she finds him. ("Been in the wars, have you?") Challenge the children to recall where they have heard these words before: it is what Millie said to Bertie when they first met (on page 64).

The White Prince and A Miracle, A Miracle!

In these two chapters, Millie continues her story, recounting how she and Bertie found the white lion and returned with it to England.

Look at the character of the French café owner and encourage the children to explain the importance of this minor figure in the story (he tells Bertie and Millie what has happened to the white lion) and what they notice about the way he speaks (in imperfect but understandable English).

Ask the children to describe how, on page 100, the author handles the reunion of Bertie and the lion, a climax in the story. Note in particular that there is a moment's uncertainty when the lion pads towards them with 'a terrible rumble in his throat'.

Examine the words Millie uses on page 106 to describe this reunion: 'amazing, surreal, almost, but… no surprise'. Why is each appropriate?

Speculate about what Bertie and Millie mean when they agree that they have 'somewhere in mind' for the lion to live. What/where is this 'somewhere'? What does it seem to suggest about Bertie and Millie? (That they will get married and live in the big house.)

The Butterfly Lion

Millie concludes her story here by summarising the rest of her life with Bertie and how they carved the shape of a lion into the chalk hillside as a memorial.

Confirm that the children understand this crucial aspect of the story: *What did Millie and Bertie do to remember the lion? Why is the lion on the hillside sometimes white and sometimes blue?*

And the Lion Shall Lie Down with the Lamb and Adonis Blues

The two final chapters, in which the boy takes up the story again and describes his return to the school, provide two major revelations or twists in the tale. Ensure that the children are aware of the narrative shift at this point. Ask them who is telling the story now. (The boy.)

After reading to the end of the novel, ask: *What two big surprises do you get?* (That the boy is called 'Morpurgo', and so, in some way, the author of the novel; that the old lady who told him the story has been dead for ten or twelve years.) Explore the implications of the second of these. How, for example, can a reader explain the boy's meeting with the old lady? Did he imagine it? Was she a ghost? (Note that the author leaves the question open.) *What special meaning does her story have for the boy and how does it change him?* (The similarities between his situation and Bertie's make it highly personal and give it a special resonant power. He is better able to 'stick out' his difficulties; he has a promise to keep – just as Bertie did. It was a story that he needed to hear.)

Shared reading

Extract 1

● This extract, from the beginning of the fourth chapter, illustrates techniques Michael Morpurgo uses to heighten the vividness and drama of a scene and to provoke a response in readers.

● Read the extract, then ask the children to summarise the action that takes place in it. This could be stated in few words, so challenge the children to sum it up as briefly as they can. Then encourage them to examine how the author makes the scene exciting and involving.

● Work with the children to highlight words and phrases used to describe movement, particularly at high speed, such as 'jumped', 'scattering', 'in a flash', 'leaping', 'racing', 'charged', 'hurled' and 'bolted', in contrast with the hyenas 'beginning to circle' and 'sidling'. Discuss these vivid and powerful word choices that help the reader to visualise the scene in detail and become involved in it.

● Notice the use of short sentences at the end of the second paragraph, which increase the pace and create drama and suspense.

● Note how the author creates uncertainty by holding back information: the rifle shot is described before the identity of the person firing it.

Extract 2

● Examination of this extract will help the children to understand the narrative structure of the novel.

● Ask the children who is telling the story at the end of the chapter that begins this extract. (The old lady/Millie.) *Who is telling the story at the beginning of the next chapter?* (The boy/Morpurgo.)

● Elicit that the novel consists of different stories told by different people – principally the story about Bertie told to the boy by the old lady, and the story about the boy which he tells himself.

● Ask the children to identify the point in the extract at which the old lady resumes her story (after the asterisks). Confirm these narrative shifts by asking children to say who the word 'I' refers to at various points in the text.

● Discuss why the author tells the story like this, with more than one narrator. For example, it adds interest and prompts involvement; it lets the reader see events from different first-person points of view.

Extract 3

● This extract forms part of the description of the first meeting of Bertie and Millie. It demonstrates how dialogue can be used as a particularly efficient way to convey characters' emotions and indicate the relationship between them.

● Ask the children to summarise what is happening in this part of the story. (Millie and Bertie are becoming friends.) How do the children know? Encourage the children to focus on the sharing of personal experiences and feelings, and on the description of the characters' behaviour as they talk, in particular Bertie's tears, his pulling at the grass and sucking at the clover, Millie's inability to express her sorrow, and the final companionable silence. *What do these details tell us about the two characters and how they are feeling?*

● Track through the extract again to note how the text shifts between dialogue, reporting of what was said and description of behaviour.

Extract 1

One morning, a week or so later, Bertie was woken by a chorus of urgent neighing. He jumped out of his bed and ran to the window. A herd of zebras was scattering away from the waterhole, chased by a couple of hyenas.

Then he saw more hyenas, three of them, standing stock still, noses pointing, eyes fixed on the waterhole. It was only now that Bertie saw the lion cub. But this one wasn't white at all. He was covered in mud, with his back to the waterhole, and he was waving a pathetic paw at the hyenas who were beginning to circle. The lion cub had

nowhere to run to, and the hyenas were sidling ever closer.

Bertie was downstairs in a flash, leaping off the veranda and racing barefoot across the compound, shouting at the top of his voice. He threw open the gate and charged down the hill towards the waterhole, yelling and screaming and waving his arms like a wild thing. Startled at this sudden intrusion, the hyenas turned tail and ran, but not far. Once within range Bertie hurled a broadside of pebbles at them, and they ran off again, but again not far. Then he was at the waterhole and between the lion cub and the hyenas, shouting at them to go away. They didn't. They stood and watched, uncertain for a while. Then they began to circle again, closer and closer…

That was when the shot ran out. The hyenas bolted into the long grass, and were gone. When Bertie turned round he saw his mother in her nightgown, rifle in hand, running towards him down the hill.

Extract 2

As the last of Table Mountain vanished in a heat haze, he said goodbye to Africa and was not at all unhappy. He had his mother with him, for the time being at least. And after all, England was nearer France than Africa was, much nearer.

Strawbridge

The old lady drank her tea and wrinkled her nose in disgust. "I'm always doing that," she said. "I'm always letting my tea go cold." The dog scratched his ear, groaning with the pleasure of it, but eyeing me all the time.

"Is that the end then?" I asked.

She laughed and put down her cup. "I should say not," she said. And then she went on, picking a tea leaf off the tip of her tongue. "Up till now it's been just Bertie's story. He told it to me so often that I feel I was there when it happened. But from now on it's my story too."

"What about the white lion?" I had to know, "Did he find the white lion? Did he keep his promise?"

The old lady seemed suddenly clouded with sadness. "You must remember," she said, putting a bony hand on mine, "that true stories do not always end just as we would wish them to. Would you like to hear the truth of what happened, or shall I make something up for you just to keep you happy?"

"I want to know what really happened," I replied.

"Then you shall," she said. She turned from me and looked out of the window again at the butterfly lion, still blue and shimmering on the hillside.

****

Whilst Bertie was growing up on his farm in Africa with his fence all around, I was growing up here at Strawbridge in this echoing cold cavern of a house with its deer park and its high wall all around.

Text © 1996, Michael Morpurgo; Illustrations © 1996, Christian Birmingham.

Extract 3

That whole afternoon we sat together on Wood Hill and he told me all about Africa, about his farm, about his waterhole, about his white lion and how he was somewhere in France now, in a circus and how he couldn't bear

to think about him. "But I'll find him," he said fiercely. "I'll find him somehow."

To be honest, I wasn't sure how much I really believed all this about a white lion. I just didn't think lions could be white.

"But the trouble is," he went on, "even when I do find him, I won't be able to take him home to Africa like I always wanted to."

"Why not?" I asked.

"Because my mother died." He looked down and pulled at the grass beside him. "She had malaria, but I think she really died of a broken heart."When he looked up his eyes were swimming with tears. "You can, you know. Then my father sold the farm and married someone else. I never want to go back. I never want to see him again, never."

I wanted to say how sorry I was about his mother, but I couldn't find the right words to say it.

"You really live here, do you?" he said. "In that big place? It's as big as my school."

I told him what little there was to know of me, all about Father being away in London so much, about Nolips and Nanny Mason. He sucked at the purple clover as I talked; and when neither of us had anything more to say we lay back in the sun and watched a pair of mewing buzzards wheeling overhead. I was wondering what would happen to him if he got caught.

Text © 1996, Michael Morpurgo; Illustrations © 1996, Christian Birmingham.

Plot, character and setting

Questions, questions

> **Objective:** To identify features that writers use to arouse reactions in their readers.
> **What you need:** Copies of *The Butterfly Lion*, mini whiteboards or jotters and pens, flipchart or board.

What to do

● Carry out this activity as soon as you have read the first page of the novel.
● Ask the children: *What questions does this first page raise for you?* Encourage immediate reactions, then give the children time to re-read the text, identify any further questions and, if you wish, record them.
● Pool ideas, collecting questions on the board: What can a 'butterfly lion' be? What is the 'it' referred to in 'I didn't dream any of it'? Why mustn't the narrator forget? Who is the 'them' referred to in 'I promised them I wouldn't'? Who is the 'I' telling the story?
● Prompt the children to offer ideas about why the author generates so many questions in the reader

right at the start of the story. What effect does this have on the reader? Draw out the idea that it arouses curiosity and prompts active involvement.
● Switch the focus to the information that *is* provided by asking what we *do* we find out from this page. For example, the narrator is looking back at his/her youth; he/she has made a promise. *What clues does this page give to what the story is going to be about and what kind of story it is going to be?* Discuss that there is a likely to be an element of mystery, suggested by the enigmatic 'butterfly lion' and the assertion that it was not a dream; it will involve a child; promises will feature; things *must* be remembered.

> **Differentiation**
> **For older/more confident learners:** Challenge children to identify at least four questions and to be ready to share them in accurately constructed sentences.
> **For younger/less confident learners:** Ask children to look for questions related to who is going to be in the story.

When did it happen?

> **Objective:** To notice and use signals of sequence and time that give coherence to a narrative.
> **What you need:** Copies of *The Butterfly Lion*, mini whiteboards or jotters and pens, flipchart or board.

What to do

● After reading the chapter entitled 'Timbavati', ask the children to recall the key events of it in sequence.
● Focus on the phrase 'One evening' at the bottom of page 26. Establish that this tells the reader when an event happened.
● Ask pairs of children to look back over pages 26–31 to find as many others words and phrases as they can that signal time, and to record them on their whiteboards or jotters.
● Then work through this section of the story as a class, collecting words and phrases in the order they occur. As well as the frequently recurring

'then' and 'when', note: 'while the lioness drank', 'came to see him later,' 'the next evening', 'a week or more passed', 'already upstairs', 'all night', 'all day', 'every day', 'never'.
● Discuss the importance in storytelling of providing the reader with clear signals of the passage of time and the sequence of events.
● You could extend the activity by asking the children to write two sentences describing the school day that include words and phrases indicating time.

> **Differentiation**
> **For older/more confident learners:** In addition, ask children to think of and record other words and phrases that indicate time and sequence.
> **For younger/less confident learners:** Limit the amount of re-reading needed by asking children to look at page 29 only. Challenge them to find at least three examples.

Plot, character and setting

The First World War

Objective: To interrogate a text to deepen and clarify understanding and response; to recognise real events that provide background to fiction.
What you need: Copies of *The Butterfly Lion*, large sheets of paper, pens or pencils, flipchart or board.
Cross-curricular links: History.

What to do

● Before reading the chapter 'A Lot of Old Codswallop', ask the children what they know about the First World War. Record key ideas on the board.
● When they have read this and the next chapter, ask pairs of children to identify and discuss new things they have learned about the war from the story. Tell them then to choose two that could be added to the list on the board, and to write a sentence for each.

● Pool ideas. You could ask questions to focus attention on significant areas, for example *What do we learn about life in France at this time? … about how wounded soldiers were cared for? How did soldiers feel about the war?*
● Talk about the idea that although *The Butterfly Lion* is fiction, it includes accurate information.
● Relate the war to other aspects of the story, including plot and character development, by asking: *What do we learn in these chapters about Bertie? …about Millie?*

Differentiation
For older/more confident learners: Ask children to find information about different aspects of the war, and to write a sentence for each.
For younger/less confident learners: Ask children to focus on pages 81–7 only. They could omit the recording part of the activity.

Bertie and the boy

Objective: To infer characters' feelings and interpret their personalities.
What you need: Copies of *The Butterfly Lion*, photocopiable page 15, pens or pencils.

What to do

● The children will need to have read most of the book before tackling this activity.
● Introduce the activity by asking the children to think of words to describe Bertie and the boy. Briefly share ideas.
● Organise the class into pairs and distribute the photocopiable sheet. Explain that they need to discuss the statements, to agree if they are true or false, and to record reasons and evidence in note form. Point out that there is not always one right answer. If they cannot make up their minds, they could write 'not sure', but encourage them to explain why they are uncertain.

● When children have completed the activity, discuss each statement in turn as a class. Prompt children to put forward reasons and evidence to support their views. Look for opportunities to re-read parts of the text and to consider whether it provides supporting evidence.
● Explore the idea that both Bertie and the boy are complex characters; some things about them are clear and unequivocal, such as Bertie's love of freedom, but others are more debatable.

Differentiation
For older/more confident learners: Encourage children to look for evidence in different parts of the story, and if appropriate to make lengthier notes on a separate sheet of paper.
For younger/less confident learners: Ask children to find one incident to support their decision about the truth or falsity of each statement – or one on each side of the argument if they are undecided.

Plot, character and setting

Events in order

> **Objective:** To identify and make notes about the main points of a text.
> **What you need:** Copies of *The Butterfly Lion*, photocopiable page 16, scissors; the events from photocopiable page 16 on an interactive whiteboard, or enlarged card versions that you can shuffle and fix on a board, plus some blank cards.

What to do

● Explain that each sentence on the photocopiable page describes an incident in the story. Ask the children to put them in the order in which they actually happened in time. Extend the task with the differentiated activities suggested below.
● When all the children have finished, work as a class to put the statements in the right order. *Which one have you put first?* (Bertie sees a white lion cub at the waterhole.) *And next?*

● Add to your list on the board the events that younger children have suggested (see below). Confirm with the class the correct position in the sequence of each one.

> **Differentiation**
> **For older/more confident learners:** Give children a second copy of the photocopiable page and ask them to say which of the events listed comes first *in the book*. (The boy runs away from school). Let them arrange the remaining incidents in the order in which they are reported in the book. Notice that there are differences between this and the *chronological* order of events. Discuss why they are different. Why does the author do it like this? (It builds suspense and involvement; it enables the author to hold back information and so on.)
> **For younger/less confident learners:** Give children two slips of paper. Ask them to recall and write down two other key events from the story and to insert them into the sequence on the photocopiable page.

Decisions, decisions

> **Objective:** To empathise with characters; to debate moral dilemmas portrayed in texts.
> **What you need:** Copies of *The Butterfly Lion*, photocopiable page 17, pens or pencils.
> **Cross-curricular links:** PSHE and citizenship.

What to do

● The children will need to have finished reading the book before they do this activity.
● Choose a decision point in the story and describe it in simple terms, such as *Bertie's father decides to sell the white lion cub to a circus.* Organise the children into pairs and ask them to identify and talk about other points when a character makes a decision. Challenge them to explain the reasons for the decision and to suggest what it tells us about the person making it. *What are the consequences?*
● Distribute the photocopiable page to pairs of children. Check that they understand that when

the have matched characters and decisions, they should choose three to talk about and be ready to share their ideas.
● Ask a pair to talk about one of their chosen ideas. Invite others who have discussed the same decision to contribute too. Has everyone understood that the decisions about running away and returning to school apply to both Bertie and the boy?
● Encourage the children to empathise with the characters and consider alternatives: *What other choice could the character have made? What might have happened then?* Share ideas as a class.

> **Differentiation**
> **For older/more confident learners:** Ask children to focus on an answer to the question *What does this tell us about the character?*
> **For younger/less confident learners:** Ask children to write sentences with a 'because' clause: 'X decided to… because…'.

Plot, character and setting

Time and space

Objective: To examine and identify the settings of a text in space and time.
What you need: Copies of *The Butterfly Lion*, large sheets of plain paper, pens or pencils, flipchart or board.

What to do
● Although *The Butterfly Lion* is a short novel, the reported action takes place over a large time span (from about 1910 to the recent past) and is set in several places (a farm in Africa; a school, a chalk hill and an old house in England; a battlefield, a hospital and a village in France). This activity gives children a way of exploring this range.
● First simply ask: *Where is the story set?* Begin to record ideas, identifying the three countries, but do not develop these in more detail. Instead, organise half the class into small groups to continue work on this. Let them choose one setting and describe it in more detail either by drawing or in words

(or both). Encourage the children to make reference to relevant parts of the text.
● Now organise the other half of the class into groups. Ask these groups: *How long does the action of the story last?* Note that there are two answers to this question. (The second answer is 'about 24 hours' – from the Sunday afternoon when the boy runs away to the Monday afternoon when he goes to the hillside.)
● When the children have completed these tasks, ask them to share their ideas: the 'settings' groups describe places in the story; the 'time' groups give the two answers and explain how they worked them out.

Differentiation
For older/more confident learners: Set these children the more challenging 'time' task.
For younger/less confident learners: Set these children the 'settings' task and get them started on it before asking the question about how long the story lasts.

Who tells whom?

Objective: To examine the use of narrators in a text.
What you need: Copies of *The Butterfly Lion*, photocopiable page 18, pens or pencils.

What to do
● This activity focuses on the use of multiple narrators in the story . Carry it out when children have finished reading the book.
● Introduce the activity by looking again at one of the short interludes that interrupt Millie's story, for instance at the beginning of 'Strawbridge' or 'A Lot of Old Codswallop'. Identify the two narrators, and discuss how the telling of the story is shared around other characters too.
● Briefly explain the task set on the photocopiable page: to say how different characters learned of different events or information.
● When the children have finished, share and

confirm answers. Choose one or two, and look together at the relevant section of the text.
● Prompt the children to discuss the effect of using different narrators in this way, contrasting it with more conventional styles of storytelling in which all or most of the information comes from the 'omniscient author' or a single first-person narrator. Suggest that the technique is way of adding interest, immediacy and realism to a story and of creating suspense.

Differentiation
For older/more confident learners: Ask children to write two more questions for the photocopiable page, using the same format, and to challenge others to answer them.
For younger/less confident learners: Provide a page reference for each question to help children find the relevant part of the story.

READ & RESPOND: Activities based on The Butterfly Lion

Bertie and the boy

Are these statements about Bertie and the boy true (**T**) or false (**F**)? Give evidence and reasons for your answer.

Bertie likes to be alone. _____

_____

_____

T / F

The boy keeps changing his mind. _____

_____

_____

T / F

Bertie wants to be free. _____

_____

_____

T / F

Bertie always keeps his promises. _____

_____

_____

T / F

The boy is always imagining things. _____

_____

_____

T / F

Bertie and the boy are very different characters. _____

_____

T / F

Events in order

Cut out the cards and put these events in the order in which they happened.

Bertie goes to school in England.	The boy meets Millie.
Bertie rescues two wounded soldiers.	Bertie meets Millie.
The boy runs away from school.	Bertie runs away from school.
Bertie tells his parents that he has seen a white lion cub at the waterhole.	Bertie and Millie take the white lion to England.
Bertie's mother scares away the hyenas.	The white lion cub is taken away to the circus.
Bertie and Millie find the circus owner.	

Decisions, decisions

Cut out the cards and match the characters to the things they decide to do.
Choose three decisions to talk about.

Bertie	**The Boy**
Millie	To run away from school.
To go with the old lady to her house.	To set the white lion free.
To go to France to look for Bertie.	To go back to school.
To carve the shape of the lion on the hillside.	To join the army.
To keep the lion on the hillside white.	

Plot, character and setting

Who tells whom?

Circle the correct answer.

1. Who tells the boy how Bertie met the white lion?

Bertie's father	Millie	the circus owner

2. How does Millie find out that Bertie won the VC?

from a newspaper	from Bertie	from the café owner

3. How does the boy find out that there is a memorial to Bertie in the school chapel?

from Millie	from Mr Cook	from a newspaper

4. Who tells Millie that the white lion was taken to the circus?

the circus owner	the boy	Bertie

5. How do Millie and Bertie find out that the circus owner killed all his animals except the white lion?

from a poster	from a newspaper	from the café owner

Illustration © 1996, Christian Birmingham.

SCHOLASTIC
www.scholastic.co.uk

READ & RESPOND: Activities based on The Butterfly Lion

Interviewing Bertie

> **Objective:** To present events and characters through dialogue to engage the interest of an audience.
> **What you need:** Copies of *The Butterfly Lion*, two chairs and a small table, notebooks, pens or pencils

What to do

● Set the scenario for this activity: Bertie is being interviewed by a radio news reporter. Tell the children to identify major episodes in his life, for example keeping the white lion, making the carving in the chalk hillside.
● Organise children into pairs, taking roles as Bertie and the reporter. Ask them to choose an episode, and give them time to prepare for the interview. Encourage them to refer to the text. (As there are several wartime incidents – including rescuing wounded comrades, time in hospital, finding the white lion and taking it back to England – it might be best to encourage

children to focus on just one.)
● Let the pairs role-play the interview, without an audience. Then give them time to review. Did the questions miss out anything important? Could the answers be more detailed or interesting? Did any answers lead into a new question?
● Choose pairs to present their interviews for the class, covering the range of episodes. Invite members of the audience to ask questions 'from the floor'.

> **Differentiation**
> **For older/more confident learners:** Encourage 'reporters' to ask searching questions, focusing on Bertie's feelings and motives. Expect those in role as Bertie to draw on the text to give detailed answers.
> **For younger/less confident learners:** Draw pairs together to focus on the same episode. Work with them to identify possible questions and to develop fuller answers.

How do they feel?

> **Objective:** To use the language of possibility to investigate and reflect on feelings, behaviour and relationships.
> **What you need:** Copies of *The Butterfly Lion*, photocopiable page 22 on card, scissors.

What to do

● Focus in on the point in the story (pages 44–5) when Bertie's father tells him that the white lion cub is going to be sold to a zoo. Ask the children how they think Bertie feels at that moment. Encourage the children to suggest a variety of words to describe his emotions. Prompt them to explain the reasons for these feelings, drawing on information from earlier in the story.
● Organise the class into small groups and distribute the photocopiable page. Check that the children understand the activity: to suggest moments when the statement on the card is

true and explain why. Stress that there is not just one right answer; the idea is to discuss how characters feel at different points in the story and to support ideas with explanation and evidence from the text.
● When the groups have had time to discuss several statements, choose one and share ideas about it as a class. Ask one group: *What moment or moments in the story have you chosen? Why?* Then ask the class: *Who agrees/disagrees?* Repeat with other statements.

> **Differentiation**
> **For older/more confident learners:** Encourage children to think of other more precise words to describe the emotion a character is feeling: 'betrayed', 'desperate', 'overjoyed'.
> **For younger/less confident learners:** Prompt groups to suggest other moments in the story where a statement applies, and to discuss why the character feels this way.

Talk about it

What's going on?

> **Objective:** To use drama strategies to explore a story.
> **What you need:** Copies of *The Butterfly Lion,* a clear space.

What to do

● If the children are unfamiliar with it, explain and demonstrate 'freeze-frame' as a drama technique: individuals or a group plan and present a 'mimed' still image that illustrates a moment in a story.

● Organise the class into pairs or groups of three. Ask them to choose a significant moment in the story and then to plan a freeze-frame image of it. Talk through the issues involved in doing this: What characters are included? Where will they be positioned in relation to each other? What body shape will each have? Explain they will need to think about how each character feels and what the relationships between them are.

Demonstrate this by presenting a one-person freeze-frame yourself and/or a two-person one with a confident child.

● Give groups time to agree on a moment from the story and to prepare and rehearse the freeze-frame image.

● Invite groups to present their freeze-frames to the class. Ask the 'audience' to say what moment in the story is being represented. Discuss the characters' emotions and relationships and how effectively these have been conveyed. Experiment with changing the position of the characters.

> **Differentiation**
> **For older/more confident learners:** Ask children to prepare a sequence of two or three freeze-frame moments to show how an incident develops.
> **For younger/less confident learners:** Suggest a few moments in the story and talk through the planning decisions.

What do you think?

> **Objective:** To offer reasons and evidence for their views, considering alternative opinions.
> **What you need:** Copies of *The Butterfly Lion,* photocopiable page 23, pens or pencils, flipchart or board.

What to do

● Choose one of the statements on the photocopiable page, or a similarly debatable point, and ask the children to discuss it briefly in pairs. Ask who agrees or disagrees with your statement and why. Prompt children to explain their opinion and support it with evidence from the story. Record reasons and evidence for and against on a two-column chart on the board.

● Organise the class into groups and ask them to use the photocopiable page to discuss other statements about the story. If you wish, appoint one member of each group to act as scribe, recording points for and against. Emphasise

that the idea is not necessarily to come to an agreement as a group, but to share ideas.

● When groups have had time to discuss all or most of the statements, choose one to debate as a class. Start by asking those who agree to put forward reasons and evidence in support of the statement; then ask others to make the opposing case. Encourage the children to refer to the detail of the story. Afterwards, ask: *Which points for and against are the strongest? Why? Is anyone changing their mind?*

> **Differentiation**
> **For older/more confident learners:** Encourage children to challenge or qualify each other's ideas, for example by arguing that a reason or piece of evidence is weak.
> **For younger/less confident learners:** Join in, asking questions that prompt children to give reasons and put forward evidence, and directing them to relevant aspects of the story.

Talk about it

Bertie Andrews, you're on tv!

Objectives: To create roles showing how behaviour can be interpreted from different viewpoints.
What you need: Copies of *The Butterfly Lion*, paper, pens or pencils, a large space with chairs set out as for the television programme *This is Your Life*, a clip of the programme (optional, and depending on your licences).

What to do

● Explain the format of television biography programmes such as *This is Your Life* in which people who know the subject (usually a famous person, but not always a 'celebrity') talk about his or her life and how they featured in it. These guests speak before they are seen and are often presented as a surprise. If possible, show an extract from *This is your life*.
● Ask the children to imagine an episode of a biography programme about Bertie. *Who would be brought on to talk about him?* (Include minor characters in the story: Nanny Mason, the colonel, the café owner, the circus owner.)

What parts of his life would they talk about? Explain the role of the host, who narrates the subject's life and interviews the guests.
● Divide the class into groups of about eight and ask them to plan and rehearse the programme about Bertie. Explain that they need to begin by assigning roles and then do some research, reviewing relevant sections of the book, to decide what each guest will say about Bertie.
● Ask groups to use the 'studio set' to present their programmes to the rest of the class – the studio audience.

Differentiation
For older/more confident learners: Ask children to write notes for their contributions. Encourage them to follow the format of the programme.
For younger/less confident learners: Support the group in making the necessary decisions. Help them to organise the presentation by taking the role of host yourself.

Who am I?

Objective: To describe characters by their individual traits, personalities and feelings; to identify the characters.
What you need: Copies of *The Butterfly Lion*, photocopiable page 24, scissors.

What to do

● Set up small groups and distribute the photocopiable page. Talk through how to play the game. Each player takes a card and then thinks about the character shown on it and the clues they can give. Explain that these clues should be in the first person, as if characters are talking about themselves. Discuss ways of making the clues 'tricky', for example by choosing features that apply to more than one character, such as 'I

am French' or 'I ran way from school'.
● Let the children play the game independently.
● Then play variations of the game as a class, perhaps with visual clues showing the character in action, or dialogue clues using words that a character speaks: 'I've set him free' (Bertie), 'I'll take you to Africa' (Millie). Include characters not shown on the photocopiable page.

Differentiation
For older/more confident learners: Challenge children to include a wider range of characters and to focus clues in particular ways, such as how characters' look, their relationships with other characters.
For younger/less confident learners: Join the game for one or two turns, then leave children to play independently.

How do they feel?

Cut out the cards. Shuffle them and put them face down in a pile.
Take the top card and read out the sentence. Talk about it with your group.
When does the character feel like this? Why?

Bertie feels angry.	Bertie feels happy.
Millie feels sad.	Bertie is worried.
Millie feels happy.	Bertie feels sad.
Bertie is surprised.	Millie is worried.
Bertie is miserable.	

What do you think?

Cut out these statements.

Discuss them and sort them into three piles:

Agree	Disagree	Not sure

Note on the back of the card why you and your group think as you do.

Bertie's father is cruel to him.	The story has a happy ending.
Bertie was wrong to take the lion cub into the house.	Bertie and the boy have a lot in common.
The boy is very different at the end of the story.	Another good title for the story would be *Born Free*.
The boy did not really meet the old lady.	

Talk about it

Who am I?

Cut out the cards. Turn them upside down and take a card each.
Think about the character you have picked.
Give the other players three clues. Don't make them too easy!
If the others don't guess correctly in three attempts, you win the card.

The boy/'Morpurgo'	**The circus owner**
Bertie's father	**Bertie's mother**
Millie	**The café owner**

■SCHOLASTIC
www.scholastic.co.uk

Get writing

'I want to keep him'

> **Objective:** To infer characters' feelings; to use role-play to explore characters' feelings.
> **What you need:** Copies of *The Butterfly Lion*, photocopiable page 28, pens or pencils.

What to do

● Pause during reading to carry out this activity when children have read the chapter 'Bertie and the lion'.

● Review the section (pages 37–9) in which Bertie's mother and father argue about whether to let him keep the lion cub. What views does each of them have on this question? What reasons do they put forward for holding these views? Which one changes his or her mind? Why do they eventually agree that Bertie can keep the lion? Encourage the children to explore these questions in depth, drawing on what they have learned about the family, and going beyond the short conversation presented on page 38. Ask them to consider what else they might have said.

● Organise the children into pairs to role-play the argument and its resolution as Bertie's parents.

● Distribute the photocopiable page and ask the children, working individually and independently, to record what Bertie's mother and father think about the question of keeping the lion. Remind them to draw on the previous discussion and role play.

● Choose some of this work to share with the class, highlighting examples where children have used inference to look more deeply at the parents' thoughts and feelings.

> **Differentiation**
> **For older/more confident learners:** Encourage children to develop the parents' thoughts in depth, for example by following a line of reasoning or linking ideas. Ask them also to focus on why Bertie's father changes his mind.
> **For younger/less confident learners:** Children could record thoughts more simply by stating each character's view and giving one reason for it.

Dear Bertie… Dear Millie

> **Objectives:** To empathise with characters; to write in role.
> **What you need:** Copies of *The Butterfly Lion*, paper (for letter-writing), pens or pencils.

What to do

● Children should try this activity when they have read as far as page 74, at which point Bertie has gone to college but not yet joined the army.

● Re-read the paragraph on page 73 beginning 'Now we did write…' and ask: *What do you think they wrote about in their letters? What events did they describe? What thoughts and feelings did they express?* To answer these questions, the children will need to think back over the relationship that has developed between Bertie and Millie, the experiences they have shared, and how they feel about the situations in which they find themselves.

● Let children write a letter from Bertie to Millie or from Millie to Bertie.

● Give all the children an opportunity to share the letters they have written by reading them aloud to a partner.

● Then choose examples to share as a class. Lead a discussion of the letters, focusing on the question, *Do you think this is what Bertie/Millie might have written?* Encourage the children to refer back to the text to support their comments.

> **Differentiation**
> **For older/more confident learners:** Children could write an exchange of letters between Bertie and Millie, perhaps in the different styles on pages 73–4.
> **For younger/less confident learners:** Encourage children to focus on what Bertie might say about his life at the college (page 74) or what Millie might say about her life at home (pages 70–71).

Get writing

In his own words

Objective: To explore characterisation and point of view; to write in role, expanding on an event from the story.
What you need: Copies of *The Butterfly Lion*, paper, pens or pencils, flipchart or board.

What to do
● Try this activity when children have read to the end of the chapter entitled 'Strawbridge'.
● Tell the children to focus on Bertie by asking: *What have been the main events in his life so far? What do we know about him?* Record key ideas, noting in particular his experiences in Africa, his being sent to a boarding school in England and his meeting with Millie.
● Shift attention to the way the story is told by considering how we know these things about Bertie. (Bertie told Millie and Millie tells the boy.) *What might be different if we learned about them in Bertie's own words, not Millie's?*

There might be, for example, more personal detail and more insight into Bertie's thoughts and feelings.
● Choose a relatively small incident in Bertie's life and use shared writing strategies to draft a short first-person account. Highlight the personal features noted above and the use of personal pronouns 'I', 'me', 'my' and so on.
● Ask the children to imagine that Bertie kept a diary. Their task is to choose another incident from the story and to write Bertie's diary entry for that day.
● Share and discuss examples of work.

Differentiation
For older/more confident learners: Encourage children to describe Bertie's thoughts and feelings in detail.
For younger/less confident learners: Let children rehearse orally first, perhaps by working in pairs to improvise conversations between Bertie and a friend. They could then write a short account inside a speech bubble.

In the news

Objective: To write non-narrative texts using structures of different text types.
What you need: Copies of *The Butterfly Lion*, photocopiable page 29, a printed news story on a specific event, paper, pens and pencils.

What to do
● Read the news story with the children. Identify key features (headline, opening sentence giving the gist of the story, photograph and caption) and their purpose (to catch and hold the reader's attention).
● Look at the headline quoted on page 110 of *The Butterfly Lion*: "The British lion comes home". Ask the children what the news report under this headline would be about. Review the relevant events (Bertie's bravery in rescuing his wounded comrades, his own injuries, the story of the white lion and Bertie's return with it to England). Draw out the literal and figurative

senses of the word 'lion' in this context. Work together to draft possibilities for an attention-grabbing first sentence.
● Ask the children to use the photocopiable page to write their own version of the news story. Remind them to use the genre features characteristic of this kind of journalistic writing.
● Share and discuss examples of work. Check that the stories give an accurate account of events and are written in a way that catches and holds a reader's attention.'

Differentiation
For older/more confident learners: Ask children to think of an alternative headline and to use the typical newspaper structure where events are not fully chronological.
For younger/less confident learners: Children could write just the opening sentence followed by two or three more, each describing a key event.

Get writing

Albert Andrews VC, 1897–1968

> **Objective:** To identify and make notes of the main points of a text, focusing on one character.
> **What you need:** Copies of *The Butterfly Lion*, extracts from appropriate obituaries, paper, pens or pencils, flipchart or board.

What to do

● For this activity, the children need to have read at least as far as page 117.

● Explain the word 'obituary' and read a few sentences from some examples. Tell the children that you want them to write an obituary for Bertie. Give them time to think of three key events in his life, then collect ideas on the board, putting them in chronological order. Check that the list includes his childhood in Africa, education in England, wartime exploits, return to England and marriage to Millie. Note that because obituaries are short, but cover the whole of the subject's life, there is no room for detail –

the focus is on significant moments.

● Explain that obituaries often begin with a summary of the subject's achievements and qualities and end with a mention of surviving family members. Use shared writing strategies to experiment with drafting these sections.

● When the children have finished, let them review their own and others' work, focusing on the questions. *Does it include the most important events in Bertie's life? Is it accurate? Does it give a clear impression of what he was like?*

> **Differentiation**
> **For older/more confident learners:** Ask children to begin with summaries of Bertie's life and to include some description of his character.
> **For younger/less confident learners:** Encourage children to recount Bertie's life in a series of short, simple sentences, such as 'Albert Andrews was born in Africa. He lived on his parents' farm…'.

Review

> **Objective:** To interrogate a text to deepen and clarify understanding and response; to write a review.
> **What you need:** Copies of *The Butterfly Lion*, photocopiable page 30, pens or pencils.

What to do

● Organise the children into pairs or small groups to share ideas about *The Butterfly Lion*. Ask some open-ended questions, such as *Did you enjoy the story? What did you like about it?*

● After five minutes or so, begin to pool ideas as a class. Gradually guide the children to focus on and develop particular aspects of the novel: plot, setting, characters, how the story is told.

● Explain that you want them to plan and write a review of *The Butterfly Lion* that children of about their own age will find interesting and useful. (If appropriate, remind the children of previous work on book reviews.)

● Distribute enlarged copies of the photocopiable page and model how to use it to make notes for a review, focusing on one section. Make sure the children understand that they should provide information about the book and express their own opinion.

● Give the children time to make notes and plan their review, before asking them to move on to write the review itself.

● Share examples. Does the review give a good idea of what the book is about and what it is like? Does it show what the reviewer thinks about the book?

> **Differentiation**
> **For older/more confident learners:** Encourage children to focus on the themes of the book, and on the structure and its effect.
> **For younger/less confident learners:** ask children to write just one sentence about each aspect of the book covered on the photocopiable page.

'I want to keep him'

Bertie's mother and father have different ideas about keeping the white lion cub.
Write down what they might be thinking.

Bertie's father

Bertie's mother

Illustrations © 1996, Christian Birmingham.

In the news

Use this layout to write a news story about Bertie's return to England.

headline _____

_____

_____

_____

_____

_____

_____

_____

photograph

_____

_____

_____

_____

_____

_____

_____

_____

Caption_____

_____   _____   _____

_____   _____   _____

_____   _____   _____

Quote(s)_____   _____

_____   _____   _____

_____   _____   _____

_____   _____   _____

_____

_____   _____   _____

Get writing

Review

Use this sheet to plan a review of *The Butterfly Lion*. Remember to write in short notes. Write your review on a separate sheet.

Introduction: What is the book about? What is it like as a 'read'?

Plot and setting: What happens? Where? What is your favourite part? Why?

Characters: Who is in the story? What are they like? Who is your favourite?

Narration: Who tells the story? How are things described?

Conclusion: Who do you think would like this book?

Assessment

Assessment advice

Although the element of adventure makes it instantly appealing and accessible, *The Butterfly Lion* is at the same time a multi-layered story with an unusual narrative structure; its themes and resonances take some puzzling out and some reflection. Focusing on the following aspects of the story will help you assess how far the children have understood and responded to the book's deeper meanings:

● How the story is told, its structure: different narrators, which events they recount in what order, how this maps on to the chronological sequence.

● Echoes and similarities: qualities that Bertie and the boy share, how the boy's meeting with Millie repeats her first meeting with Bertie.

● Themes: freedom (for animals and humans), sticking things out and keeping promises, loneliness and unhappiness, remembrance.

● Characters: their feelings at various points, why they behave as they do, the dilemmas and crises they face, how they change.

The things people say

> **Objective:** To understand the significance of words spoken by characters in the story.
> **What you need:** Photocopiable page 32, pens or pencils.

What to do

● At various points in *The Butterfly Lion*, characters say something that means more than it would appear to at first sight, something that suggests underlying themes. An illuminating way of assessing children's understanding of the story and characters is to ask them to explain the significance of these utterances.

● Hand out the photocopiable page and ask the children to write down who speaks the words and to whom, and to explain why these words are important in the story. (Alternatively, the task could be carried out orally, using the sheet to structure a discussion with an individual child or a small group.)

● In assessing the children's work, look for responses that show understanding of and response to the deeper significance of what characters say and of how this relates to the story's themes.

● Millie to the boy (page 17). Millie's words of advice suggest the importance in the story of determination and commitment – of relevance not just to the boy, but also to Bertie, Millie and the circus owner.

● Bertie to the lion cub (page 48). The keeping of this promise during Bertie and Millie's lifetimes and beyond is the unifying idea and plotline of the story.

● Bertie's mother to his father, about keeping the lion cub (page 38). Her words suggest the interdependence and neediness of characters, and particularly that the need is not just one way; seen further not just in Bertie's family, but also in his relationship with Millie and in Millie's relationship with the boy.

● Millie to Bertie (page 67, and echoed almost word for word in her conversation with the boy on page 119). One of the points at which the similarities between Bertie and the boy are clearest.

● Millie to the boy (page 119). Words that suggest the impact on the boy of his encounter with Millie: he can return to it as a source of strength. Does it perhaps also hint at what will be revealed about the reality of the meeting?

● Mr Cook to the boy (page 122). A revelation that raises doubt, and further intrigue, about the reality of the boy's meeting with Millie.

The things people say

Who speaks these lines? To whom are they speaking?
Why are their words important in the story?

- "You've got to stick it out, see things through."

_____

_____

- "All my life I'll think of you, I promise I will. I won't ever forget you."

_____

_____

- "He needs us, and maybe we need him."

_____

_____

- "You've got to go back, before they miss you."

_____

_____

- "I may not always be easy to find, but I'll be here."

_____

_____

- "She died only a few months later. Broken heart, they say. You can you know. You can die of a broken heart."

_____

_____